AF334059

To Celebrate

Date

THANK YOU FOR COMING.

Let's celebrate!

SPACE FOR A PHOTO

Guest Name

Wishes & Messages

Email/Phone

Guest Name

Wishes & Messages

Email/Phone

Guest Name

Wishes & Messages

Email/Phone

Guest Name
Wishes & Messages
Email/Phone

Guest Name

Wishes & Messages

Email/Phone

Guest Name

Wishes & Messages

E
Email/Phone

Guest Name
Wishes & Messages
Email/Phone

Guest Name

Wishes & Messages

Email/Phone

Guest Name
Wishes & Messages
Email/Phone

Guest Name

Wishes & Messages

Email/Phone

Guest Name

Wishes & Messages

Email/Phone

Guest Name
Wishes & Messages
Email/Phone

Guest Name

Wishes & Messages

Email/Phone

Guest Name

Wishes & Messages

Email/Phone

Guest Name

Wishes & Messages

Email/Phone

Guest Name

Wishes & Messages

Email/Phone

Guest Name

Wishes & Messages

Email/Phone

Guest Name

Wishes & Messages

Email/Phone

Guest Name
Wishes & Messages
Email/Phone

Guest Name

Wishes & Messages

Email/Phone

Guest Name

Wishes & Messages

Email/Phone

Guest Name
Wishes & Messages
Email/Phone

Guest Name
Wishes & Messages
EMAIL/PHONE

Guest Name

Wishes & Messages

Email/Phone

Guest Name

Wishes & Messages

Email/Phone

Guest Name

Wishes & Messages

Email/Phone

Guest Name
Wishes & Messages
Email/Phone

Guest Name
Wishes & Messages
Email/Phone

Guest Name

Wishes & Messages

Email/Phone

Guest Name

Wishes & Messages

Email/Phone

Guest Name
Wishes & Messages
Email/Phone

Guest Name

Wishes & Messages

Email/Phone

Guest Name
Wishes & Messages
Email/Phone

Guest Name

Wishes & Messages

Email/Phone

Guest Name

Wishes & Messages

Email/Phone

Guest Name

Wishes & Messages

Email/Phone

Guest Name

Wishes & Messages

Email/Phone

Guest Name

Wishes & Messages

Email/Phone

Guest Name

Wishes & Messages

Email/Phone

Guest Name

Wishes & Messages

Email/Phone

Guest Name
Wishes & Messages
Email/Phone

Guest Name
Wishes & Messages
Email/Phone

Guest Name

Wishes & Messages

Email/Phone

Guest Name

Wishes & Messages

Email/Phone

Guest Name

Wishes & Messages

EMAIL/PHONE

Guest Name

Wishes & Messages

Email/Phone

Guest Name
Wishes & Messages
Email/Phone

Guest Name

Wishes & Messages

Email/Phone

Guest Name

Wishes & Messages

Email/Phone

Guest Name

Wishes & Messages

EMAIL/PHONE

Guest Name
Wishes & Messages
Email/Phone

Guest Name

Wishes & Messages

Email/Phone

Guest Name

Wishes & Messages

Email/Phone

Guest Name

Wishes & Messages

Email/Phone

Guest Name

Wishes & Messages

Email/Phone

Guest Name
Wishes & Messages
Email/Phone

Guest Name

Wishes & Messages

Email/Phone

Guest Name

Wishes & Messages

Email/Phone

Guest Name
Wishes & Messages
Email/Phone

Guest Name

Wishes & Messages

Email/Phone

Guest Name

Wishes & Messages

Email/Phone

Guest Name

Wishes & Messages

Email/Phone

Guest Name

Wishes & Messages

Email/Phone

Guest Name
Wishes & Messages
Email/Phone

Guest Name

Wishes & Messages

Email/Phone

Guest Name

Wishes & Messages

Email/Phone

Guest Name

Wishes & Messages

Email/Phone

Guest Name

Wishes & Messages

Email/Phone

Guest Name

Wishes & Messages

Email/Phone

Guest Name

Wishes & Messages

Email/Phone

Guest Name
Wishes & Messages
Email/Phone

Guest Name

Wishes & Messages

Email/Phone

Guest Name

Wishes & Messages

Email/Phone

Guest Name
Wishes & Messages
Email/Phone

Guest Name

Wishes & Messages

Email/Phone

Guest Name

Wishes & Messages

Email/Phone

Guest Name
Wishes & Messages
Email/Phone

Guest Name

Wishes & Messages

Email/Phone

Guest Name

Wishes & Messages

Email/Phone

Guest Name
Wishes & Messages
Email/Phone

Guest Name
Wishes & Messages
Email/Phone

Guest Name

Wishes & Messages

Email/Phone

Guest Name

Wishes & Messages

Email/Phone

Guest Name

Wishes & Messages

Email/Phone

Guest Name

Wishes & Messages

Email/Phone

Guest Name

Wishes & Messages

Email/Phone

Guest Name

Wishes & Messages

Email/Phone

Guest Name

Wishes & Messages

Email/Phone

Guest Name

Wishes & Messages

EMAIL/PHONE

Guest Name

Wishes & Messages

Email/Phone

Guest Name

Wishes & Messages

Email/Phone

Guest Name

Wishes & Messages

Email/Phone

Guest Name

Wishes & Messages

EMAIL/PHONE

Guest Name

Wishes & Messages

Email/Phone

Guest Name

Wishes & Messages

Email/Phone

Guest Name
Wishes & Messages
Email/Phone

Guest Name

Wishes & Messages

Email/Phone

Guest Name

Wishes & Messages

Email/Phone

Guest Name

Wishes & Messages

Email/Phone

Guest Name

Wishes & Messages

Email/Phone

Guest Name
Wishes & Messages
Email/Phone

Guest Name

Wishes & Messages

Email/Phone

Guest Name

____

Wishes & Messages

____

____

____

____

____

____

Email/Phone
____

Guest Name
Wishes & Messages
Email/Phone

Guest Name

Wishes & Messages

Email/Phone

GIFT LOG

Name /Email /phone	Gift

GIFT LOG

Name /Email /phone | Gift

GIFT LOG

Name /Email /phone	Gift

GIFT LOG

Name /Email /phone	Gift

GIFT LOG

Name /Email /phone	Gift

GIFT LOG

Name /Email /phone	Gift

GIFT LOG

Name /Email /phone	Gift

NOTES & PHOTO

NOTES & PHOTO

NOTES & PHOTO

NOTES & PHOTO

NOTES & PHOTO

NOTES & PHOTO

NOTES & PHOTO